Scholastic Su...

BRAIN PLAY™

1st-3rd Grade

2ND EDITION

Workbook

NEW YORK • TORONTO • LONDON • AUCKLAND • SYDNEY

MEXICO CITY • NEW DELHI • HONG KONG • BUENOS AIRES

■ SCHOLASTIC

Acknowledgements

From *Get Ready for 1st Grade*. Published by Scholastic Teaching Resources/Scholastic
Inc. Copyright © 2004 by Scholastic Inc. Reprinted with permission.

From *Get Ready for 2nd Grade*. Published by Scholastic Teaching Resources/Scholastic
Inc. Copyright © 2004 by Scholastic Inc. Reprinted with permission.

From *Get Ready for 3rd Grade*. Published by Scholastic Teaching Resources/Scholastic
Inc. Copyright © 2004 by Scholastic Inc. Reprinted with permission.

ISBN 0-545-05208-4

8 9 10 23 11 10 09 08 07 06

Table of Contents

READING COMPREHENSION

Trucks

 *The **main idea** tells what the whole story is about.*

Trucks do important work. Dump trucks carry away sand and rocks. Cement trucks have a barrel that turns around and around. They deliver cement to workers who are making sidewalks. Fire trucks carry water hoses and firefighters. Gasoline is delivered in large tank trucks. Flatbed trucks carry wood to the people who are building houses.

Find the sentence in the story that tells the main idea. Write it in the circle below. Then draw a line from the main idea to all the trucks that were described in the story.

Gorillas

 Details *are parts of a story. Details help you understand what the story is about.*

Gorillas are the largest apes. They live in the rainforests of Africa. Every morning, they wake up and eat a breakfast of leaves, fruit, and bark. During most of the day, the adult gorillas take naps. Meanwhile, young gorillas play. They wrestle and chase each other. They swing on vines. When the adults wake up, everyone eats again. When there is danger, gorillas stand up on their hind legs, scream, and beat their chests. Every night before it gets dark, the gorillas build a new nest to sleep in. They break off leafy branches to make their beds, either on the ground or in the trees. Baby gorillas snuggle up to their mothers to sleep.

Find the answers to the puzzle in the story. Write the answers in the squares with the matching numbers.

Across

1. During the day, adult gorillas _____.

3. Gorillas eat leaves, bark, and _____.

5. The largest apes are _____.

7. In danger, gorillas beat their _____.

8. Young gorillas swing on _____.

Down

2. The continent where gorillas live is _____.

4. When young gorillas play, they _____ and chase each other.

6. Baby gorillas snuggle up to their mothers to _____.

What's for Lunch?

Have you ever had a string bean sandwich? Most students wouldn't want that for lunch! What is the favorite sandwich in America's school lunches? If you said peanut butter and jelly, you'd be right. Other popular sandwiches are ham and bologna. Cheese is the fourth favorite sandwich. Many students also like turkey sandwiches.

What is the topic of the paragraph?
Write it in the center circle.
Find five details that tell about the topic.
Write them in the web.

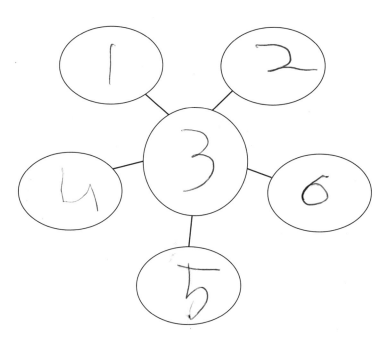

Fancy Fireworks

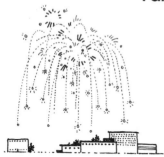

Kaboom! It's the Fourth of July. Fireworks light up the night. Have you ever seen a willow firework? It has long trails of color that float to the ground. The pinwheel and comet are two other popular fireworks. One of the loudest fireworks is called the salute. After a bright flash, you hear a loud BOOM!

Read the paragraph. Then answer the questions.

1. Which firework has long trails of color?

_____

2. Which firework makes a loud BOOM?

_____

3. What is a popular firework?

_____

A Stormy Day

Big, black clouds appeared in the sky. Lightning struck the tallest tree. The scared cow cried, "Moo!" It rained hard. Soon there was a mud puddle by the barn door. Hay blew out of the barn window.

Read the story above. Then go back and read each sentence again. Add to the picture everything that the sentences describe.

Who Am I?

 Use details from the story to make decisions about the characters.

Circle the picture that answers the riddle.

1. I have feathers. I also have wings, but I don't fly. I love to swim in icy water. Who am I?

2. I am 3 weeks old. I drink milk. I cry when my diaper is wet. Who am I?

3. I live in the ocean. I swim around slowly, looking for something to eat. I have six more arms than you have. Who am I?

4. I am an insect. If you touch me, I might bite you! I make tunnels under the ground. I love to come to your picnic! Who am I?

5. I am a female. I like to watch movies and listen to music. My grandchildren love my oatmeal cookies. Who am I?

6. I am a large mammal. I live in the woods. I have fur. I stand up and growl when I am angry. Who am I?

7. I wear a uniform. My job is to help people. I ride on a big red truck. Who am I?

Where the Sun Shines

Florida is known for its pleasant weather. In fact, it has earned the nickname "Sunshine State." As a result of its warm, sunny climate, Florida is a good place for growing fruits, such as oranges and grapefruits. Many older people go to live in Florida. They enjoy the good weather. Northerners on vacation also visit Florida for the same reason.

Read the paragraph. Then complete the cause-and-effect map.

Effects

Cause

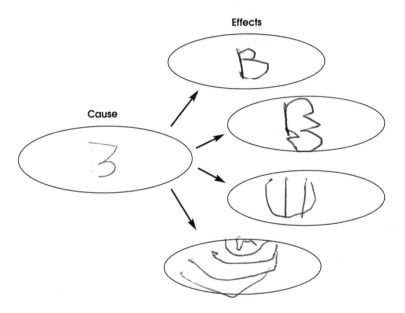

Foreign Flags

Every country has its own flag. Japan has a white flag with a red circle on it. The red circle stands for the sun. Japan's name means the "land of the rising sun." Canada also has a red and white flag. But its flag has a white background with two wide red stripes. In the center of the flag is a red maple leaf. The maple tree is a symbol of Canada.

Read the paragraph. Then answer the questions.

1. What colors are both flags? _____

2. What does Japan's flag have in the center? _____

3. What does Canada's flag have in the center? _____

4. How are the backgrounds of the two flags different? _____

Write your answers in the correct parts of the circles.

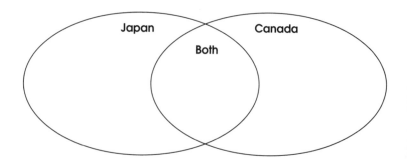

Japan   Canada

Both

Story Comprehension

Read the story. Then answer each question.
Fill in the bubble next to the best answer.

> Cats and dogs are good pets. You can find these pets in many homes.
>
> A cat is a good pet. A cat can run and jump. A cat can play with a ball of yarn. A cat can also lick your hand.
>
> A dog is a good pet, too. A dog can chase after a ball. A dog can jump up and catch a stick. A dog can also help keep you safe.

1. What two animals make good pets?

   O cats

   O dogs and sharks

   O dogs and cats

2. What is a good title (name) for this story?

   O Good Pets

   O Cats at Home

   O Pet Food

3. What can both cats and dogs do?

   O jump up and catch a stick

   O keep you safe

   O run and jump

Whales

Read the story. Then answer each question.
Fill in the bubble next to the best answer.

A whale is a very big animal. Whales live in the sea. Some whales swim with each other. They travel in large groups, called pods. They swim around, looking for food.

Whales feed on sea life. Some whales eat plants. Other whales have teeth and can eat seals and small fish.

Whales must stay wet all the time. However, they also must come to the top of the sea to breathe. When a whale leaps out of the water to catch a breath of air, it is an amazing sight.

1. What are pods?
   - O whale food
   - ● groups of whales
   - O sea animals

2. What is a good title (name) for this story?
   - O The Sea
   - O Fish
   - ● Whales

3. What must all whales do?
   - O eat seals and fish
   - O spend time on land
   - ● stay wet

4. Why do whales sometimes jump out of the water?
   - O to warm up
   - ● to get air
   - O to catch fish

Letter From Vera

April 11

Dear Morey,

I just got your letter with the picture of you riding your bike. From the smile on your face, I can tell how much fun you're having. I still remember when you could hardly ride a tricycle. You've come a long way!

Now here's some advice. I'm sure you're a good rider. But you will fall off that bike now and then. So please get yourself a helmet. Wear it every time you ride. A helmet will help protect you from a head injury. Wearing a helmet when you ride a bike is as important as wearing your seat belt when you ride in a car!

No, I'm not trying to be a bossy know-it-all. I just don't want a bad fall to wipe that smile off your face. When you come to visit this summer, bring your bike and your helmet. We'll take some great rides together!

Your cousin,
Vera

1. **From this letter, what can you tell about the picture of Morey that he sent to Vera?**

    A. He is riding a tricycle.   C. He is in his driveway.

    B. He is not wearing a helmet.   D. He is looking scared.

2. **Vera's advice shows that she:**

    E. cares a lot about safety.   G. doesn't like riding bikes.

    F. is often bossy and mean.   H. is learning to drive a car.

3. **What will Morey do with Vera during the summer?**

    _____

    _____

    _____

Blending In

How are the following words alike: *blue, black, blink*? If you said they all begin with *bl*, you're right. Some other words that begin with these letters are *blob, blanket*, and *blimp*. Letter pairs like *bl* are blends. Blends are two or more consonants that work together. What blend do the following words begin with: *green, gray, grumpy*? Two other blends are *tr* and *sm*. Words such as *smoke, smile, try, tray, smack, trick, truck*, and *smell* begin with these blends.

Use the paragraph to write four headings for the chart. Then write examples under each heading.

GRAMMAR

Capitalize First Word

Read each sentence. Then fill in the circle next to the word with the capital letter that begins the sentence.

1. **The cat is in the van.**

   ⭕ cat

   ⭕ The

2. **My dog can run.**

   ⭕ My

   ⭕ dog

3. **Jan can hop.**

   ⭕ Jan

   ⭕ hop

4. **I like ham.**

   ⭕ ham

   ⭕ I

5. **Ants like jam.**

   ⭕ jam

   ⭕ Ants

People, Places, and Things

Common nouns name people, places, or things.
Read each sentence. Circle the common nouns.

1. The boy made a boat.

2. The brothers went to the park.

3. A girl was with her grandmother.

4. Two boats crashed in the lake.

5. Friends used a needle and thread
    to fix the sail.

Capitalize Names and Places

Special names of people and places always begin with capital letters. They are called **proper nouns.**

Read the postcard. Find the proper nouns. Write them correctly on the lines below.

Dear sue,

    It's very hot here in california. We visited the city of los angeles. Then we swam in the pacific ocean. I miss you.

            Love,

            tonya

sue wong

11 shore road

austin, texas 78728

1. _____   2. _____

3. _____   4. _____

5. _____   6. _____

7. _____   8. _____

More Than One

Many nouns, or naming words, add **-s** to show more than one.

Read the sets of sentences. Draw a line under the sentence that has a naming word that names more than one.

1. Jan has her mittens.

   Jan has her mitten.

2. She will run up a hill.

   She will run up hills.

3. Jan runs with her dogs.

   Jan runs with her dog.

4. The dogs can jump.

   The dog can jump.

Look at each picture. Read each word. Write the plural naming word that matches the picture.

5.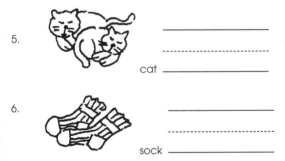

cat _____

6.

sock _____

Adding Words

A **compound noun** is made up of two smaller words put together.

cup   **cake**   **cupcake**

Can you figure out what these compound nouns are?
Read the clues. Then write the compound noun.

1. A **cloth** that covers a **table** is a _____

2. **Corn** that goes **pop** is _____

3. A **book** for a **cook** is a _____

4. An **apple** made into **sauce** is _____

5. A **cake** with **fruit** in it is a _____

6. **Meat** made into a **ball** is a _____

7. A **melon** with lots of **water** in it is a _____

8. A **berry** that is **blue** is a _____

Action at the Game

A **verb** is an action word. It tells what someone or something is doing.

Draw a line to match each sentence with an action verb. Then write the action verbs on the lines to finish the sentences.

1. Moms and dads _____ the game.   throws

2. The pitcher _____ the ball.   opens

3. Ronald _____ his eyes.   watch

4. The team _____ for Ronald.   cheers

5. Ronald _____ the ball past the pitcher.   runs

6. He _____ to first base.   hits

7 Someone _____, "Go, Ronald, go!"   eat

8. The kids _____ ice cream after the game.   yells

How to Agree

If the naming part of a sentence is a noun or pronoun that names one, the verb ends in **-s**, except for the pronouns **I** and **you**. If the naming part is a noun or pronoun that names more than one, the verb does not end in **-s**.

Read each sentence. Circle the correct verb to complete it.

1. John and his family (camp, camps) in the woods.

2. Alice (like, likes) hiking the best.

3. John (walk, walks) ahead of everyone.

4. Mom and John (build, builds) a campfire.

5. Dad and Alice (cook, cooks) dinner over the fire.

6. Alice and Mom (crawl, crawls) into the tent.

Action Words

Verbs tell when action takes place. Present-tense verbs tell about action that is happening now. A verb showing the action of one person ends in **-s**. A verb telling the action of more than one person does not end in **-s**.

The boy sings.   The boys sing.

In the sentences below, underline each action verb.

1. **Four birds sit on the fence.**

2. **That dog digs.**

3. **A man sells hotdogs.**

4. **The girls run.**

Verb or Noun?

The meaning of a word often depends on how the word is used.
Some words can be used as both verbs and nouns.

Add the word at the left to each sentence pair. Write verb or noun on
the line next to each sentence to show how you used the word.

peel   1. The _____ is the cover of an orange.   _____

2. The students _____ their oranges.   _____

ride   3. Jan's _____ on the camel was bumpy. _____

4. People _____ on camels in the desert. _____

34

color   5. The twins _____ their pictures.   _____

        6. That _____ fades in the sun.   _____

smell   7. The men _____ smoke.   _____

        8. The _____ of flowers fills the air.   _____

lock   9. The _____ on the box is old.   _____

       10. The Turners _____ their door at night. _____

A Verb Puzzle

Verbs tell when action takes place. Past-tense verbs tell about action that happened in the past. Most past-tense verbs end in **-ed**.

Write the past tense of each word in the box. Then use the past tense words to complete the puzzle below.

call _____	mix _____	play _____
yell _____	kick _____	help _____
bark _____	climb _____	walk _____

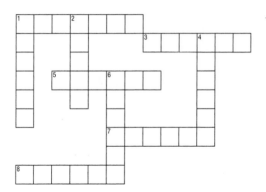

Across

1. Mike _____ over the wall.

3. The dog _____ .

5. Our teacher _____ us with the math problems.

7. We _____ at the team to win.

8. The boys _____ home from school.

Down

1. Sam _____ his dad on the phone.

2. Grandma _____ the cake batter.

4. The player _____ the ball.

6. Marie _____ a game with Zack.

Describe a Noun

An **adjective** describes a person, place, or thing. Color, size, and number words are adjectives.

Read each sentence. Find the adjective and the noun it describes. Circle the noun. Write the adjective on the line.

1. Peggy and Rosa went to the big zoo.   _____

2. They looked up at the tall giraffe.   _____

3. The giraffe looked down at the two girls.   _____

4. The giraffe had brown spots.   _____

Write adjectives from the sentences in the chart.

Color Word	Size Words	Number Word
_____	_____	_____
	_____	

Describing a Surprise

Use adjectives to describe an object.

Read the words on the box.
What do they describe?

_____

| white | high |
| puffy | moving |

Think of a surprise to hide in each box. Then write four adjectives to describe it.

1.

2.

3.

4.

Contractions With *not*

A **contraction** is two words made into one word. An **apostrophe** takes the place of the missing letter or letters. In a contraction, **not** becomes **n't**.

Read each sentence. Write a contraction for the underlined words.

1. Cindy and Ed <u>could not</u> bake a cake. _____

2. There <u>was not</u> enough flour. _____

3. They <u>are not</u> happy. _____

4. <u>Do not</u> give up! _____

5. They <u>did not</u> give up.
   They made cupcakes! _____

Send In the Subs

A **pronoun** is a word that can take the place of a noun.

The nouns in these sentences need a rest. Pick a pronoun to replace the underlined word(s). Then write the sentence with the pronoun.

Pronoun Subs				
he	you	we	it	she

1. <u>Tanya</u> swings the bat.

   _____

2. <u>Matt and I</u> warm up.

   _____

3. <u>Leo</u> looks for his glove.

   _____

4. <u>The ball</u> rolls into the field.

   _____

Check your sentences. Did you begin them with a capital letter?

Patriotic Sentences

Color the flag to show:

RED = sentence   WHITE = not a sentence

★ ★	This is a flag.
	The flag
	The flag has stars.
	The stars
	The stars are white.
	The stripes
	The stripes are red.

And white
The stripes are white.
Blue part
The flag has a blue part.
There are
There are 50 stars.

Who Does It?

The **subject** of a sentence tells who or what did something.

Read the sentences below. Look at the picture to find out who or what is doing the action described in the sentence and then write it on the line.

1. A _____ sits in the wagon.

2. A _____ rides in the wagon too.

3. _____ is pulling the wagon.

4. Her _____ wants a ride too.

5. The _____ can carry all the animals.

6. The _____ fly along with them.

What Happens?

The **predicate** of a sentence tells what happens.

For each sentence, write an ending that tells what is happening in the picture.

1. The cat _____.

2. A mouse _____.

3. The cat _____.

4. The mouse _____.

Mixed-Up Words

Words in a sentence must be in an order that makes sense.

These words are mixed up. Put them in order. Then write each sentence.

1. snow. bear likes This

    _____

    _____

    _____

    _____

    _____

2. water cold. The is

    _____

    _____

    _____

    _____

    _____

3. fast. The runs bear

_____

_____

_____

_____

_____

4. play. bears Two

_____

_____

_____

_____

_____

Hop to It!

A telling sentence begins with a capital letter and ends with a period.

Rewrite each sentence correctly.

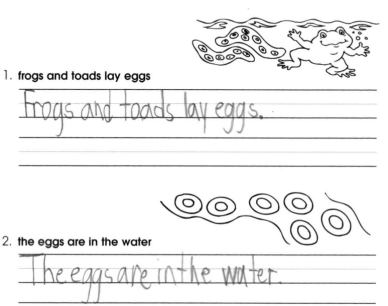

1. **frogs and toads lay eggs**

Frogs and toads lay eggs.

2. **the eggs are in the water**

The eggs are in the water.

3. tadpoles hatch from the eggs

Tadpoles hatch from the eggs.

4. the tadpoles grow legs

The tadpoles grow legs

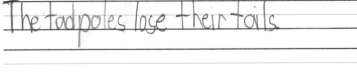

5. the tadpoles lose their tails

The tadpoles lose their tails

Exclamations and Commands

An **exclamation** is a sentence that shows strong feeling. It ends with an exclamation point. A **command** is a sentence that gives an order. It ends with a period.

A. Read each sentence. Write E on the line if the sentence is an exclamation. Write C if the sentence is a command.

1. They chase buffaloes! _____

2. You have to go, too. _____

3. Wait at the airport. _____

4. It snows all the time! _____

5. Alligators live in the sewers! _____

6. Look at the horse. _____

7. That's a great-looking horse! _____

8. Write a letter to Seymour. _____

B. Complete each exclamation and command. The punctuation mark at the end of each line is a clue.

1. I feel _____!

2. Help your _____.

3. That's a _____!

4. I lost _____!

5. Turn the _____.

6. Come watch the _____.

7. Please let me _____.

Statements and Questions

A **statement** is a sentence that tells something. It ends with a period. A **question** is a sentence that asks something. It ends with a question mark.

A. Read each sentence. Write Q on the line if the sentence is a question. Write S if the sentence is a statement.

1. Where did the ant live? _____

2. The ant had many cousins. _____

3. She found the crumb under a leaf. _____

4. How will she carry it? _____

5. Who came along first? _____

6. The lizard wouldn't help. _____

7. He said he was too cold. _____

8. Why did the rooster fly away? _____

WRITING

A–M

Trace and write the alphabet.

A B C

D E F

G H I

J K L M

N–Z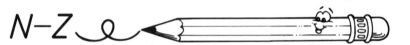

Trace and write the alphabet.

N   O   P

Q   R   S

T   U   V

W   X   Y   Z

a–m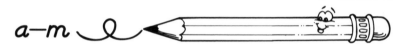

Trace and write the alphabet.

a b c

d e f

g h i

j k l m

n–z

Trace and write the alphabet.

n   o   p

q   r   s

t   u   v

w   x   y   z

Shapes

Trace and write.

oval

heart

circle

square

triangle

diamond

rectangle

Twinkle, Twinkle Little Star

Rewrite each sentence using periods.

1. **Tonight I saw a star**

   _____

   _____

   _____

   _____

   _____

2. **I saw the star twinkle**

   _____

   _____

   _____

   _____

   _____

3. **It looked like a candle**

   _____

   _____

   _____

   _____

   _____

4. **It was very bright**

_____

_____

_____

_____

_____

5. **I made a wish**

_____

_____

_____

_____

_____

6. **I hope it comes true**

_____

_____

_____

_____

_____

In Warm Weather

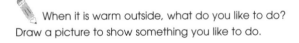 When it is warm outside, what do you like to do?
Draw a picture to show something you like to do.

When it is warm outside, I like to _____

_____

I like doing this because _____

_____

When it is warm, I like to go to _____

_____

I like warm weather because _____

_____

Ask Mother Goose

*A sentence that asks a question ends with a **question mark** (?).*
It often begins with one of these words.

Who . . .   Where . . .   Why . . .   Could . . .
What . . .   When . . .   Will . . .

Rewrite the questions using capital letters and
question marks.

1. where is the king's castle

_____

_____

2. who helped Humpty Dumpty

_____

_____

3. why did the cow jump over the moon

_____

_____

4. will the frog become a prince

_____

_____

5. could the three mice see

_____

_____

Wacky World

An asking sentence is called a **question**. It begins
with a capital letter and ends with a question mark (**?**).

Write each question correctly.

1. why is that car in a tree

_____

_____

2. should that monkey be driving a bus

_____

_____

3. did you see feathers on that crocodile

_____

_____

Sunny Sentences

 Every sentence begins with a **capital letter.**
A **telling sentence** *ends with a* **period** *(.).*
An **asking sentence** *ends with a* **question mark** *(?).*

Rewrite each sentence correctly.

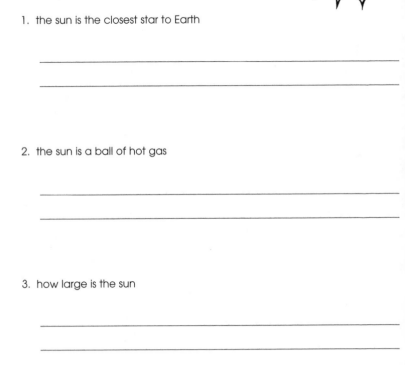

1. the sun is the closest star to Earth

_____

_____

2. the sun is a ball of hot gas

_____

_____

3. how large is the sun

_____

_____

Country Roads

A good sentence uses describing words to help the reader "paint a picture" in his or her mind.

Add a describing word from the list to finish each sentence.

1. The _____ chicken laid

   _____ eggs in her nest.

2. The _____ barn

   keeps the _____

   animals warm at night.

3. _____ carrots grow in

   the _____ garden.

4. Two _____ pigs sleep in

   the _____ pen.

5. The _____ cows drink

   from the _____ pond.

6. A _____ scarecrow

   frightens the _____ birds.

wooden

sunny

lazy

black

three

orange

thirsty

cold

shallow

muddy

funny

fat

That Sounds Fishy to Me

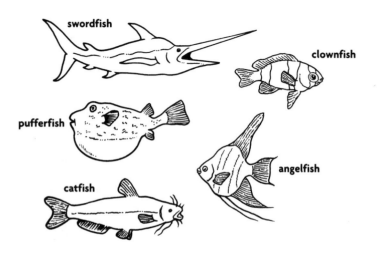

A **telling sentence** *begins with a* **capital letter** *and ends with a* **period**.

Write a sentence about each fish. Remember to tell a complete idea.

swordfish

clownfish

pufferfish

angelfish

catfish

1. The swordfish has a long snout.

2.

3.

4.

5.

Football Frenzy

A sentence is more interesting when it gives exact information.

Replace each 🏈 word to make the sentence more exact.

1. **The** ball **game starts** soon.

   The _____soccer_____ game starts _____now_____.

2. **We are meeting** her there.

   We are meeting _____ _____.

3. **Let's eat** this **and** that **before the game.**

   Let's eat _____ and _____ before

   the game.

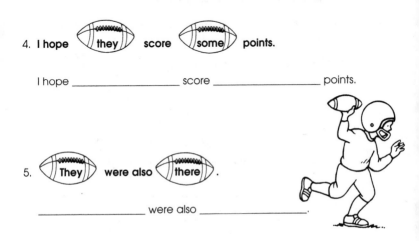

4. I hope **they** score **some** points.

I hope _____ score _____ points.

5. **They** were also **there**.

_____ were also _____.

6. **He** played a **good** game!

_____ played a _____ game!

Great Gardening Tips

Sentences can also be combined to make them more interesting. Key words can help put two sentences together.

I will plan my garden. I am waiting for spring.

I will plan my garden while I am waiting for spring.

Combine the two sentences using the key word. Write a new sentence.

1. Fill a cup with water. Add some flower seeds. and

_____

_____

2. This will soften the seeds. They are hard. because

_____

_____

3. Fill a cup with dirt. The seeds soak in water. while

_____

_____

4. Bury the seeds in the cup. The dirt covers them. until

_____

_____

MATH

Number User

I use numbers to tell about myself.

1. _____
   My Street Number

2. _____
   My Zip Code

3. _____
   My Telephone Number

4. _____
   My Birthday

5. _____

My Age

6. _____

My Height and Weight

7. _____

Number of People in My
Family

I can count up to

8. _____

Naming Shapes

1. Draw a line matching each shape to its name.

triangle

circle

square

rectangle

2. Make an X on the shape that does not belong in the row.

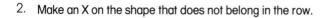

3. Which shape looks like a balloon?

4. Which shape has four corners?

5. Which shape looks like an egg?

What Comes Next?

Draw the shapes to complete each pattern.

1. ☆ ◯ ☆ ◯ ☐ ☐

2. ♡ ⇨ ♡ ⇨ ☐ ☐

3. ♡ ⇨ ☆ ♡ ☐ ☐

Pattern Learner

A **pattern** is a repeated arrangement of numbers, shapes, or lines in a row. Continue the patterns below.

1. 324, 435, 546,

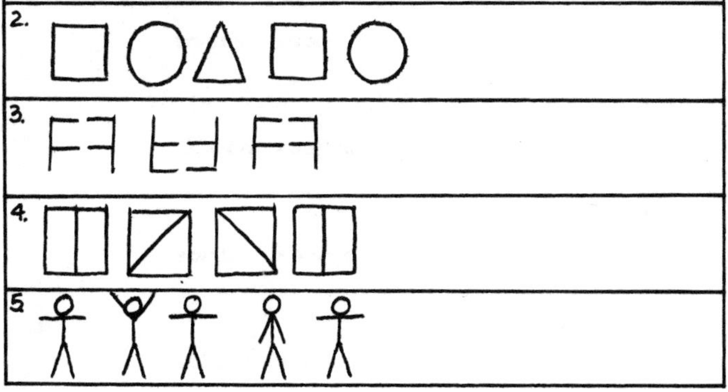

2. ☐ ◯ △ ☐ ◯

3. F⅃ � F⅃

4. ▯ ◲ ◱ ▯

5. stick figures pattern

Weight Watcher

Weight can be measured in ounces (oz.) and pounds (lb.). 16 oz. = 1 lb. Which unit of measure would you use to weigh the items below? Underline the more sensible measure.

1. An apple

   ounces   pounds

2. A pair of sneakers

   ounces   pounds

3. A bar of soap

   ounces   pounds

4. A bicycle

   ounces   pounds

5. A watermelon

   ounces   pounds

6. A baseball player

   ounces   pounds

7. A balloon

ounces   pounds

8. A jam sandwich

ounces   pounds

9. A baseball bat

ounces   pounds

10. A pair of socks

ounces   pounds

11. A slice of pizza

ounces   pounds

12. A full backpack

ounces   pounds

13. A large dog

ounces   pounds

14. A loaf of bread

ounces   pounds

15. A paintbrush

ounces   pounds

Adding 1 to 5

Solve each problem.

1.  3 + 2 = 5	4. 2 + 1 = 3
2. 4 + 0 = 4	5. 1 + 3 = 4
3. 1 + 4 = 5	6. 5 + 0 = 5

Clowning Around

Add. Color the picture
using the color code.

Color Code

1	pink
2	white
3	black
4	brown
5	purple
6	green
7	blue
8	orange
9	yellow
10	red

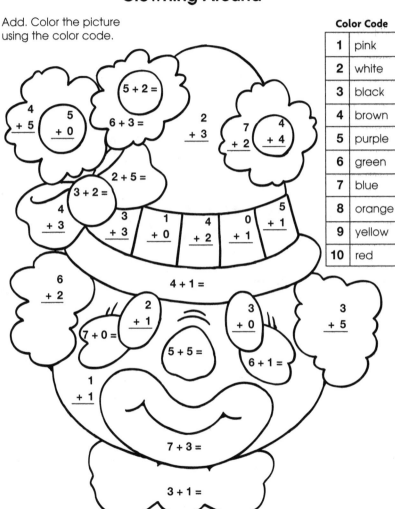

Math

Subtraction

Scarecrow Subtraction

Cross out the pictures to solve each problem.

1.

$6 - 4 = \underline{2}$

2.

$5 - 3 = \underline{2}$

3.

$6 - 1 = \underline{5}$

4. 4 crows are in the field.
   The scarecrow scares 3 of the crows away.
   How many crows are left?

   $4 - 3 = \underline{1}$

Blast Off

Add or subtract. Then use the code to answer the riddle on the next page.

$$\begin{array}{r} 3 \\ + 4 \\ \hline 7 \end{array}$$
S

$$\begin{array}{r} 9 \\ - 5 \\ \hline 4 \end{array}$$
H

$$\begin{array}{r} 8 \\ - 8 \\ \hline 0 \end{array}$$
D

$$\begin{array}{r} 6 \\ + 4 \\ \hline 10 \end{array}$$
F

$$\begin{array}{r} 7 \\ - 6 \\ \hline 1 \end{array}$$
O

$$\begin{array}{r} 6 \\ - 4 \\ \hline 2 \end{array}$$
L

$$\begin{array}{r} 2 \\ + 3 \\ \hline 5 \end{array}$$
U

$$\begin{array}{r} 2 \\ + 7 \\ \hline 9 \end{array}$$
T

$$\begin{array}{r} 8 \\ - 2 \\ \hline 6 \end{array}$$
W

$$\begin{array}{r} 4 \\ + 4 \\ \hline 8 \end{array}$$
I

$$\begin{array}{r} 10 \\ - 7 \\ \hline 3 \end{array}$$
R

How is an astronaut's job unlike any other job?

I T ' S   O U T   O F
8 9 7   1 5 9   1 10

T H I S   W O R L D !
9 4 8 7   6 1 3 2 0

Super Star

Solve the problems. If the answer is between 1 and 20, color the shape red. If the answer is between 21 and 40, color the shape white. If the answer is between 41 and 90, color the shape blue.

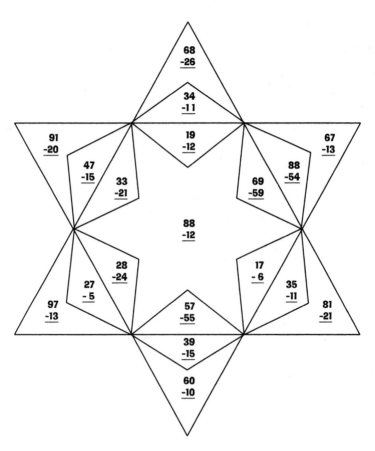

68
-26

34
-11

91
-20

19
-12

67
-13

47
-15

33
-21

88
-54

69
-59

88
-12

28
-24

17
- 6

27
- 5

35
-11

97
-13

57
-55

81
-21

39
-15

60
-10

Patterns for the Mail Carrier

Meimei the mail carrier is delivering letters. Give her some help. Fill in the missing addresses on the houses below.

Coin-Toss Addition

Toss 6 coins. Write **H** for heads or **T** for tails in the circles below to show your toss. Then write the addition equation. Write the number of "heads" first. We did the first one for you. Try it five times.

(H)(H)(H)(H)(T)(T) Equation: __4 + 2 = 6__

◯◯◯◯◯◯ Equation: _____

◯◯◯◯◯◯ Equation: _____

◯◯◯◯◯◯ Equation: _____

◯◯◯◯◯◯ Equation: _____

◯◯◯◯◯◯ Equation: _____

Number Words

Write each sentence using numbers and symbols.

1. Four plus five is nine.	
2. Eleven minus six is five.	
3. Nine plus seven is sixteen.	
4. Four plus eight is twelve.	
5. Three minus two is one.	
6. Seven plus seven is fourteen.	
7. Fifteen minus ten is five.	
8. Two plus eight is ten.	
9. Five minus two is three.	

Parts to Color

A fraction has two numbers. The top number will tell you how many parts to color. The bottom number tells you how many parts there are.

Color 1/5 of the circle.

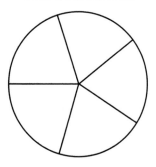

Color 4/5 of the rectangle.

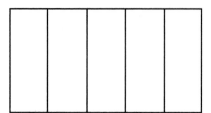

Color 3/5 of the ants.

Color 2/5 of the spiders.

Color 0/5 of the bees.

Color 5/5 of the worms.

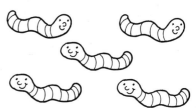

More Fun With Fractions

A fraction has two numbers. The top number will tell you how many parts to color. The bottom number tells you how many total parts there are.

A. $\frac{10}{10}$ is the whole circle.

Color $\frac{8}{10}$ of the circle.

How much is not colored? ___

B. $\frac{10}{10}$ is the whole rectangle.

Color $\frac{4}{10}$ of the rectangle.

How much is not colored? ___

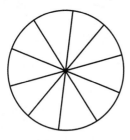

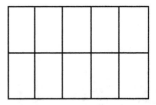

$$\frac{10}{10} - \frac{8}{10} = \underline{}$$

$$\frac{10}{10} - \frac{4}{10} = \underline{}$$

C. Solve this fraction equation. Cross out the dogs to help you.

$$\frac{10}{10} - \frac{3}{10} = \underline{\ \text{7}\ }$$

How Many Legs?

Fill in the blanks.

1.	How many legs on		
		1 turkey _____	3 turkeys _____
		2 turkeys _____	4 turkeys _____
2.	How many legs on		
		1 cat _____	3 cats _____
		2 cats _____	4 cats _____
3.	How many legs on		
		1 ladybug _____	3 ladybugs _____
		2 ladybugs _____	4 ladybugs _____

Field Trip Cars

1.

Josie's class is going to the teddy bear factory.

Three children will ride in each car.

Draw a circle around the children who will ride in each car.

How many cars do they need? _____

2.

Pete's class is going to see the elephant seals.

Five children will ride in each van.

Draw a circle around the children who will ride in each van.

How many vans do they need? _____

Adding Quickly

 The addition sentence 4 + 4 + 4 + 4 + 4 = 20 can be written as a multiplication sentence. Count how many times 4 is being added together. The answer is 5. So, 4 + 4 + 4 + 4 + 4 = 20 can be written as 5 x 4 = 20. Multiplication is a quick way to add.

Write a multiplication sentence for each addition sentence.

A. **5 + 5 + 5 = 15**

_____

B. **6 + 6 + 6 + 6 = 24**

_____

C. **8 + 8 = 16**

_____

D. **2 + 2 + 2 + 2 = 8**

_____

E. **7 + 7 + 7 = 21**

_____

F. **4 + 4 + 4 + 4 = 16**

_____

G. **9 + 9 + 9 = 27**

_____

H. **5 + 5 + 5 + 5 + 5 = 25**

_____

I. **3 + 3 + 3 + 3 + 3 = 15**

_____